# GOD'S SABBATH
## *IS THE*
# SEVENTH DAY
# OF THE WEEK
## (SATURDAY).

## METUSELA ALBERT

To order additional copies of this book, contact:
Xlibris
844-714-8691
www.Xlibris.com
Orders@Xlibris.com

Scripture quotations marked KJV are from the Holy Bible, King James Version (Authorized Version). First published in 1611. Quoted from the KJV Classic Reference Bible, Copyright © 1983 by The Zondervan Corporation.

ISBN: 978-1-6698-7149-1 (sc)
ISBN: 978-1-6698-7148-4 (e)

Print information available on the last page

Rev. date: 03/20/2023

## Exodus 20:8-11

[8] "Remember the Sabbath day, to keep it holy.

[9] Six days shalt thou labor and do all thy work;

[10] but the seventh day is the Sabbath of the LORD THY GOD. In it thou shalt not do any work, thou, nor thy son, nor thy daughter, thy manservant, nor thy maidservant, nor thy cattle, nor thy stranger that is within thy gates.

[11] For in six days the LORD MADE HEAVEN AND EARTH, THE SEA, AND ALL THAT IN THEM IS, AND RESTED THE SEVENTH DAY. Therefore the LORD BLESSED THE SABBATH DAY AND HALLOWED IT."

# Contents

# INTRODUCTION

We are in the year 2023, and we are not too far from two thousand years since the time JESUS resurrected and ascended back to heaven in 31 A.D.

Believe it or not? Most Professed Christians, Preachers, Bishops, Evangelists, and Pastors, still have <u>not</u> understood the <u>SABBATH DAY</u> of the living GOD, as written in the Ten Commandments – (Exodus 20:8-11).

Unfortunately, the subject about the SABBATH DAY of the most-high GOD, is still not being understood by most professed Christians in the 21st century.

Why is this dark veil still hanging among the Protestant Churches when the Scripture is so clear about the SABBATH day of the living GOD?

## WHY? . . . WHY? . . . WHY? . . .

## LISTED BELOW ARE NINE MAIN REASONS THAT CAUSED THE PROTESTANT CHURCHES TO OBSERVE SUNDAY AS THE SABBATH DAY INSTEAD OF SATURDAY.

Reason # 1 – They believed that the Sabbath was first given at Mt. Sinai (1,446 B.C.) through Moses, and only for the children of Israel, <u>not</u> for the Gentiles.

Reason # 2 – They believed that the Sabbath Commandment was changed at Calvary after the death of JESUS, but <u>not</u> the other nine commandments.

Reason # 3 – They believed that the resurrection day which was a Sunday should be observed instead of the Seventh day (Sabbath).

Reason # 4 – They believed that JESUS kept the law for us, and we as Born-Again Christians are free from keeping the Sabbath Commandment.

Reason # 5 – They believed that we have been forgiven and saved at Calvary by JESUS' death, thus, the Sabbath commandment is <u>not</u> a requirement to obey. This is the teaching of UNCONDITIONAL SALVATION.

Reason # 6 – They believed that Eternal life is <u>by faith only</u> without obedience to the law.

Reason # 7 – They believed that a sinner can be saved <u>in</u> sin, rather than <u>from</u> sin. In other words, one can be saved while transgressing GOD'S law.

Reason # 8 – They believed that we are in the <u>New Covenant</u> era, not the Old Covenant that was made at Mount Sinai with the Children of Israel.

Reason # 9 – They believed that it is legalistic (Pharisaic) to keep the Sabbath Commandment, but not legalistic to obey the other nine Commandments.

Reason # 10 – They believed that since JESUS kept the law perfectly and died as if he was the sinner to pay the penalty of sin, thus, we are not required to keep the law including the Sabbath day.

NOTE: They failed to explain what it means to be "IN CHRIST."

Here is the real truth. When we are "IN CHRIST" <u>(Born Again)</u>, the law will be written in our hearts and we will love to keep His law because JESUS is in our hearts.

Whenever we are <u>not</u> in Christ, we will transgress the law in <u>our hearts</u> before we transgress it outwardly. Read Matthew 5:17-19; 1 John 3:6-9.

...........................................................................................................

NOTE: The nine reasons stated above will be proven wrong in this book.

...........................................................................................................

The Bible is so clear that THE SABBATH DAY is the seventh day of the week which is Saturday, the day *before* the first day of the week (Sunday). Yes, the Sabbath day is <u>not</u> Sunday.

## LOGIC THINKING IS A MUST

Let's do the logic thinking. Since the first day of the week is <u>Sunday</u>, therefore the Sabbath has to be <u>Saturday</u>, the day *before* <u>Sunday</u>. Is this too hard to understand? This is <u>not</u> rocket science. It is logic thinking by God's grace and wisdom. It is that simple that a child can understand.

## COME AND LET US REASON TOGETHER

The weekly cycle has seven days only. Thus, the seventh day is the Sabbath day. Every other day of the week is <u>not</u> the Sabbath day.

## THERE IS NO SUCH THING AS A <u>LUNI SABBATH.</u>

Once you understood that the Sabbath day will always be on the seventh day of the week which is Saturday, then the Luni Sabbath theory where it says, the Sabbath day can fall on any day of week in different months depending on the New Moon for that month, is contradicting.

Remember, there is no such thing as a luni-Sabbath based on the appearance of the new moon every month. Actually, the luni-Sabbath theory is a Moon Worship theory, and must be rebuked and condemned.

..................................................................................................................................................

# THE PURPOSE OF THIS BOOK

This book is intended to be a text Book in the Seminaries and Bible Colleges for students and Pastors who are seeking to understand the true Sabbath day of the living GOD.

Since what you believed will affect your lifestyle, and your lifestyle will affect your destiny, thus, this book is to help shape your lifestyle and destiny. How? So that you cease transgressing the law of God – (Exodus 20:8-11; John 14:15).

If you love JESUS, then obey his law. His law includes the Sabbath day. Sunday is not the Sabbath day.

This is a book that can be used in your home Bible Study group to clarify the Sabbath day. Once you come to a good understanding of the Sabbath truth, the error is exposed.

Remember, Sunday is not the Sabbath day. JESUS rose from the grave on the first day of the week which was a Sunday, the day after the Sabbath day. The four gospels in the New Testament recorded that JESUS rose from the grave on *the first day* of the week which was a Sunday. (Matthew 28:1-5; Mark 16:1-5; Luke 24:1-6; John 20:1-5).

It is my prayer that ELOHIM / YAHWEH / JEHOVAH who commanded us to keep holy his Sabbath day as written in the Ten Commandments (Exodus 20:8-11), give you wisdom to understand this controversial subject.

This is a book that is also going to help you understand who JESUS was, is, and is to come. He is the LORD of the Sabbath – (Mark 2:27-28). He was not a Trinity God.

Dear readers, I can assure you that after reading this book, you will not believe again that Sunday is the Sabbath day of GOD nor in the Trinity GOD theory that says, 1 + 1 + 1 = 1.

JESUS was the ELOHIM / YAHWEH / JEHOVAH who created heaven and earth in six days and rested on the seventh day (Sabbath). HE was not, and is not, a Trinity GOD nor a Triune GOD.

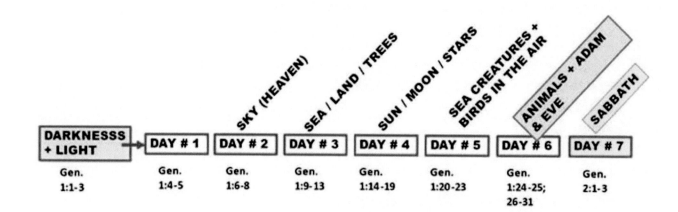

**ADAM AND EVE WERE NOT JEWS WHEN THE SABBATH WAS MADE AND GIVEN TO THEM AT CREATION– GENESIS 1:31-2:1-3.**

COMPILED BY: METUSELA F. ALBERT

**May God bless your heart for understanding this subject.**

# CHAPTER 1

# THE SABBATH WAS MADE FOR MANKIND AT CREATION.

Let's read the Scripture.

**Genesis 1:31**

And God saw every thing that <u>He</u> had made, and behold, it was very good. And the evening and the morning were <u>the sixth day</u>.

..........................................................................................................................................

**Genesis 2:1-3**

1 Thus the heavens and the earth were finished, and all the host of them.

² <u>And on the seventh day God ended His work which He had made; and He rested on the seventh day from all His work which He had made.</u>

³ And <u>God blessed the seventh day and sanctified it</u>, because in it <u>He</u> had rested from all <u>His</u> work which <u>God</u> created and made.

## THE LORD GOD OF THE SABBATH DAY WAS NOT A TRINITY GOD. READ THE CONTEXT.

- Genesis 1:31
- And God saw every thing that He had made, and behold, it was very good. And the evening and the morning were the sixth day.
- ....................................................................................................
- Genesis 2:1-3
- 1 Thus the heavens and the earth were finished, and all the host of them.
- 2 And on the seventh day God ended His work which He had made; and He rested on the seventh day from all His work which He had made.

- 3 And God blessed the seventh day and sanctified it , because in it He had rested from all His work which God created and made.

Compiled by: Metuesla F. Albert

- ....................................................................................................

When GOD created heaven and earth, he made Adam and Eve on the sixth day of the week. And on the seventh day, God rested from all his work which he had made. The seventh day was the Sabbath day.

Of course, the Sabbath day was made for Adam and Eve and all their descendants including us, to remind everyone that God made heaven and earth in six days. GOD was the Creator. Worship is due to him who created us. He is our Creator. There is only one GOD who made us. JESUS was that GOD (ELOHIM / YAHWEH / JEHOVAH).

NOTE: Adam and Eve were not Jews. Therefore, the Sabbath was not made for the Jewish people, but for all people. If you did not understand this point, then re-think until you get it. Nobody needs to be a Jew to observe the Sabbath day. Of course, nobody needs to be a Seventh Day Adventist member to observe the seventh day as the Sabbath day.

Allow me to remind us again - The Sabbath was made for mankind; the descendants of Adam and Eve, to remind us that GOD made us, and we did not evolve out of monkeys. Thus, there should be no evolution theory to be taught in the education system around the world.

> • **Mark 2:27-28 King James Version**
> • **27 And He said unto them, "The Sabbath was made for man, and not man for the Sabbath.**
> • **28 Therefore the Son of Man is Lord also of the Sabbath."**
>
> **EXPLANATION:**
> **JESUS CREATED THE SABBATH FOR ADAM AND EVE AND THEIR DESCENDANTS, TO REMIND THEM THAT IT WAS JESUS WHO CREATED EVERYTHING IN SIX DAYS. THUS, THERE SHOULD BE NO EVOLUTION TEACHING.**

## THE SABBATH DAY IS THE SEVENTH DAY OF THE WEEK.

## IT IS SATURDAY IN TODAY'S RECKONING.

The seventh day is the Sabbath day of the LORD. JESUS who is the LORD of the Sabbath day is our only GOD in heaven. HE alone created heaven and earth in six days. HE was not the Son of GOD at the time HE created heaven and earth. HE became the Son of GOD by incarnation through Mary at Bethlehem around 04 B.C.

After everything were created in six days, the LORD of the Sabbath sets aside the seventh day to be the Sabbath day. HE gave us the weekly cycle of seven days a week - (Genesis 1:31; 2:1-3). Of course, the Sabbath day on earth was first introduced to Adam and Eve at the Garden of Eden. The Sabbath was made for man, not man for the Sabbath. . . They were not Jews. I repeat again, Adam and Eve were not Jews.

Did you notice something? Adam and Eve were created on the sixth day of the week. The next day which is the seventh day (the Sabbath) was made for man (Mark 2:27-28). Of course, the Sabbath was made for Adam and Eve and their generations to follow. The Sabbath day was a memorial of Creation, not a memorial of the Resurrection. You need to understand this point well.

NOTE: The Sabbath was not made for the Jews. There was not one Jew who existed then at the Garden of Eden with Adam and Eve - (Genesis 1:27-31; 2:1-3). How many did not understand such a simple truth stated in here? Unfortunately, so many people who claimed to be believers in JESUS, still have not understood it. Perhaps, you are one. Stay tuned and keep reading.

## TRY AND UNDERSTAND THIS IMPORTANT POINT WELL.

Adam and Eve were not Seventh-day Adventists either. No Seventh-day Adventist Church existed at creation. In fact, the Seventh-day Adventist Church was only founded in May - 1863 A.D., by Mrs. Ellen G. White and her friends.

Did you not know yet? The Sabbath day was observed by the disciples – Acts 13. And JESUS observed the Sabbath day as his custom – Luke 4:16. JESUS who was the GOD of Abraham who delivered the children of Israel from slavery in Egypt, wrote the Sabbath Commandment in the Ten Commandments on two tablets of stone at Mt. Sinai – (Exodus 20:8-11; 31:18).

Therefore, nobody needs to be a Seventh-day Adventist member or a biological Jew, to keep the weekly Sabbath day. The Sabbath day of the LORD is for all mankind on earth to keep because God commanded it in the fourth commandment which is part of the Ten Commandments.

In the New Testament time, JESUS said, "If you love me, keep my Commandments." (John 14:15). Love for JESUS should be the motivating factor for us to keep the Sabbath day. It is not legalistic to love our Creator and keep his Sabbath day. After knowing the truth about the Sabbath day, and you reject the truth and replace it with another day as your Sabbath day, hence you become a transgressor of God's law. And the wages of sin - is eternal death – (Romans 6:23). It is unlawful to replace the Sabbath day by keeping another day as the Sabbath day of the living GOD.

Prior to the giving of the Ten Commandments at Mount Sinai, the generation from Adam and Eve before and after the flood, knew of the Sabbath day because it was given to Adam and Eve at creation before they sinned. This point has to be fully understood well.

Abraham kept God's commandments – (Genesis 26:5). He lived *before* the giving of the Ten Commandments at Mt. Sinai which proves that the descendants of Adam and Eve who lived before the time of Moses knew about the Sabbath day. Did you understand the point? Hope so.

You cannot separate the fourth commandment from the rest of the Ten Commandments.

You cannot choose to obey just the fourth commandment and ignore the other nine Commandments. And you cannot choose to obey the other nine Commandments and ignore the fourth commandment, as some tried to do today in the Protestant Churches.

JESUS said, "IF you love Me, keep My commandments." - (John 14:15). In case you did not know yet, JESUS was the YAHWEH (JEHOVAH) who wrote the Ten Commandments on two tablets of stone at Mt. Sinai, and gave through Moses.

Scriptures: Genesis 2:1-3; Exodus 3:13-14; 6:1-3; 20:1-17; 31:18; John 5:39, 46; 8:56-58; 14:15; Revelation 14:12; 21:6-7; 22:14.

## THE TRUTH ABOUT GOD, JESUS, AND THE HOLY SPIRIT.... ONLY ONE DIVINE BEING. NOT TWO, AND NOT THREE.

1. JESUS WAS GOD (YAHWEH / JEHOVAH) THE FATHER WHO BECAME THE SON OF GOD <u>BY INCARNATION</u> THROUGH MARY AT BETHLEHEM – (04 B.C.).

2. YAHWEH (JEHOVAH) DID <u>NOT</u> HAVE A SON CALLED – JESUS, IN HEAVEN.

3. YAHWEH (JEHOVAH) DID <u>NOT</u> HAVE A SON CALLED – JESUS, IN THE OLD TESTAMENT ERA.

4. YAHWEH (JEHOVAH) GAVE BIRTH TO NO SON CALLED – JESUS.

5. THE GOD (YAHWEH / JEHOVAH) OF ABRAHAM HAD <u>NO</u> SON CALLED JESUS.

6. SATAN WANTED TO BE LIKE GOD IN HEAVEN, NOT LIKE THE SON OF GOD BECAUSE THERE WAS NO SON OF GOD IN HEAVEN.

7. THE HOLY SPIRIT WAS THE SPIRIT OF GOD, NOT A THIRD PERSON.

Compiled by: Metusela F. Albert

---

| SLIDE # 1 | THE TIMELINE OF BIBLICAL HISTORY <u>FROM CREATION</u> TO THE TIME OF THE FLOOD |

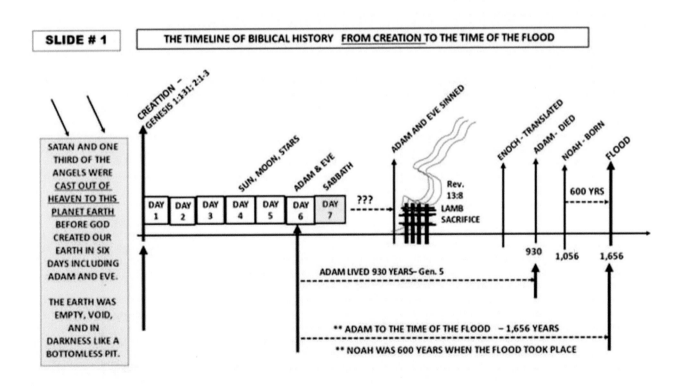

Adam and Eve were created on the sixth day of the week (Genesis 1:26-31). And the day after was the seventh day of the week (Genesis 2:1-3). The seventh day is the Sabbath day given to Adam and Eve at creation to remind them that it was God who created heaven and earth and all the hosts in six days.

The Sabbath was made for man at creation – (Mark 2:27-28). Adam and Eve were not Jews. Thus, the Sabbath was not made for the Jews. Every seventh day of the week is the Sabbath day. The weekly Sabbath is to be observed every week, which is over 50 times in a year.

Don't forget this: The weekly Sabbath is the fourth commandment in the Ten Commandments – (Exodus 20:8-11).

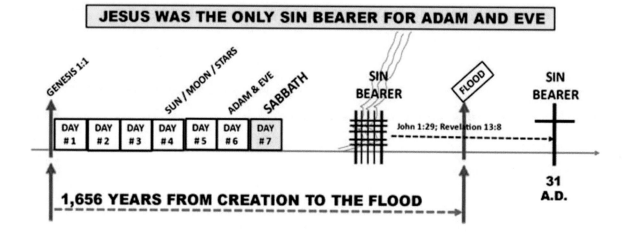

**JESUS WAS THE ONLY SIN BEARER FOR ADAM AND EVE**

Compiled by: Metusela F. Albert

## BIBLICAL FACTS ABOUT THE SABBATH DAY

1. The SABBATH day will always be on the seventh day of the week (Genesis 2:1-3).
2. The weekly cycle is only seven days.
3. Men may change the calendar, but that cannot change the SABBATH day to another day of the week.
4. The SABBATH day is the day between the 6th day and the 1st day of the week. It is between Friday and Sunday.
5. The SABBATH day is the fourth Commandment in the Ten Commandments – (Exodus 20:8-11).
6. The SABBATH day comes over 50 times in a year.
7. The SABBATH day was first given to Adam and Eve at Creation, NOT to the Jewish people – (Genesis 2:1-3).
8. The SABBATH day reminds us that GOD created heaven and earth in six days.
9. Adam and Eve were made on the sixth day, therefore, there was no such thing called – EVOLUTION. Of course, man did not evolve out of Monkeys.
10. JESUS was the LORD of the SABBATH day, the Creator.

Compiled by: Metusela F. Albert

# KEEP THIS IN MIND

The Sabbath and the Ten Commandments were <u>not</u> given for the Jews, <u>but for all mankind</u>. It is a universal law for all mankind. When you break one commandment, you have broken all commandments – (James 2:10). And we will all be judged by the Ten Commandments – (Ecclesiastes 12:13-14). The law is holy, just, and righteous – (Romans 7:12). Without the law, we would not have known what sin is – (Romans 4:15). By the law is the knowledge of sin – (Romans 3:20).

We were <u>not</u> told how long Adam and Eve lived on earth before they disobeyed God by eating the forbidden fruit, the tree of the knowledge of good and evil – (Genesis 2:16-17; 3:1-5). After Adam and Eve's disobedience, God offered himself as the atonement by a lamb that was killed as the substitute. He was the symbolic lamb slain from the foundation of the earth – (John 1:29; Revelation 13:8).

- **Genesis 2:1-3 - NKJ**
- **1. Thus the heavens and the earth, and all the host of them, were finished.**
- **2 And on the seventh day God ended His work which He had done, and He rested on the seventh day from all His work which He had done.**
- **3 Then God blessed the seventh day and sanctified it, because in it He rested from all His work which God had created and made.**

Prepared by: Metusela F. Albert

**Exodus 20:8-11 - NKJ**

8 "Remember the Sabbath day, to keep it holy.
9 Six days you shall labor and do all your work,

10 but the seventh day *is* the Sabbath of the LORD your God. *In it* you shall do no work: you, nor your son, nor your daughter, nor your male servant, nor your female servant, nor your cattle, nor your stranger who *is* within your gates.

11 For *in* six days the LORD made the heavens and the earth, the sea, and all that *is* in them, and rested the seventh day. Therefore the LORD blessed the Sabbath day and hallowed it.

**JESUS WAS THE GOD (YAHWEH) WHO MADE HEAVEN AND EARTH IN SIX DAYS AND RESTED ON THE SEVENTH DAY.**

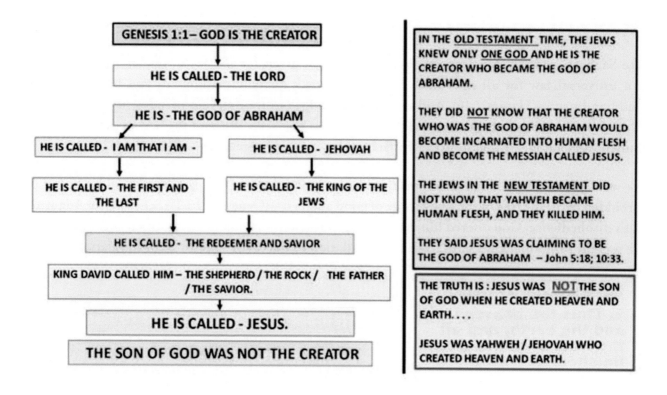

Genesis 1:31; 2:1-3; Exodus 3:13-14; 6:1-3; Isaiah 43:10; 44:6, 24; 49:16; John 5:39, 46; 8:56-58; Revelation 21:6-7.

........................................................................................................................................................

# THE SABBATH WAS <u>NOT</u> MADE FOR THE JEWS.

Remember, Adam and Eve were <u>not</u> Jewish. Thus, the Sabbath was <u>not</u> made for the Jews.

<u>We need to understand that the Jewish (Israelite) people only existed from Jacob, the grandson of Abraham.</u> Jacob's name was changed to <u>Israel</u>. He was the Father of the Israelites who ended up in Egypt and became slaves for about four hundred years until God called Moses at <u>the burning bush</u> to go and deliver them – (Exodus 3:13-14). It was the PASSOVER night that the Jews were delivered from slavery – the 14th day of the month of Nisan – (Exodus 12:1-14).

////////////////////////////////////////////////////////////////////////////////////////////////////////////////

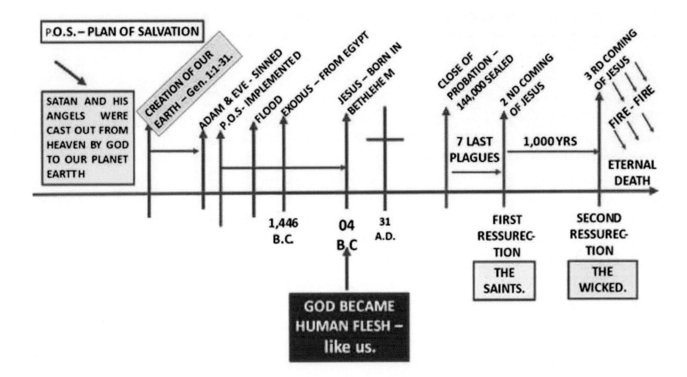

JESUS died the *first death* at the hands of the Roman soldiers at Calvary because he was human. It was his human flesh which was born of Mary at Bethlehem that died at Calvary, <u>not</u> his divinity. The divinity of JESUS did *not* die at Calvary because none can kill God.

Jesus voluntarily died the second death on the cross, as if he was the sinner so that none should die eternally. Eternal death will happen at the end of the 1,000 years, which is after the second resurrection. Therefore, No person has died the second death because the first and second resurrections have not taken place yet. Please study the chart/diagram shown above.

## A CRUCIAL POINT -

NOTE: JESUS who was the GOD (YAHWEH /JEHOVAH) of Abraham cannot die. HE was immortal. In order for YAHWEH to die as our Sin Bearer (Redeemer) to pay for the penalty of sin, he humbly took human flesh by the INCARNATION process through Mary at Bethlehem. He took a mortal body like us. He inherited the fallen sinful nature like us. He did <u>not</u> inherit sin. He inherited the first death and died at Calvary by the hands of the Roman soldiers. . . . He did <u>not</u> inherit sin nor the second death.

JESUS, while in human flesh, had two natures - the divine nature and the human nature. His divine nature did <u>not</u> die at Calvary. It was his human nature that died at Calvary.

# CHAPTER 2

# ADAM AND EVE TRANSGRESSED THE TEN COMMANDMENTS.

**Genesis 2:15-18 (King James Version)**

[15] And <u>the LORD GOD</u> took the man and put him into the Garden of Eden to dress it and to keep it.

[16] And <u>the LORD GOD</u> commanded the man, saying, "Of every tree of the garden thou mayest freely eat;

[17] but of the tree of the knowledge of good and evil, thou shalt not eat of it. For in the day that thou eatest thereof, thou shalt surely die."

[18] And <u>the LORD GOD</u> said, "It is not good that the man should be alone; I will make him a helper meet for him."

........................................................................................................................

## Genesis 3:11

[11] And He (God) said, "Who told thee that thou wast naked? Hast thou eaten of the tree whereof <u>I</u> commanded thee that thou shouldest not eat?"

........................................................................................................................

In Genesis 2:16-17, God instructed Adam and Eve <u>not</u> to eat of the tree of the knowledge of good and evil. On the day that they eat of it, they will surely die.

Sadly, Adam and Eve disobeyed God and ate of the tree of the knowledge of good and evil. As a result, God removed them from the Garden of Eden. An angel with a sword was stationed at the Garden of Eden to keep them away from eating <u>the tree of life,</u> to avoid them becoming immortal sinners. Later, Adam and Eve died. They died the first death, <u>not</u> the eternal death because JESUS became the Sin Bearer. A lamb had to die in Adam and Eve's place. That lamb was symbolic of JESUS, who later would die at Calvary, as if he was the Sinner.

# LET'S MAKE SURE WE UNDESTOOD IT WELL.

Adam and Eve's sins were transferred to JESUS, the SIN-BEARER for Adam and Eve. That is why babies are <u>not</u> the Sin-Bearer for Adam and Eve. . . No baby is born a sinner. No baby inherited Adam and Eve's sins. Sin is a choice, not without a choice. Sin is by the transgression of God's law – (1 John 3:4). Sin is <u>not</u> by the fallen sinful nature.

You are responsible for sin by your own choice. Adam and Eve are not responsible for your sins. And God is not responsible for your sins. Don't excuse your sins. If you believe that you inherited sin from Adam, then you are indirectly putting the blame upon Adam and Eve as the cause for you to sin. Therefore, you are excusing sin. And you are blaming GOD for creating you a sinner without your choice.

In other words, the doctrine called – Babies are born sinners, is Satanic. And the doctrine called – Sin is by nature, is devilish. Of course, the doctrine that says, We are sinners because of Adam' sin, must be condemned.

## Genesis 3:14-17

[14] And <u>the Lord God</u> said unto the serpent, "Because thou hast done this, thou art cursed above all cattle, and above every beast of the field. Upon thy belly shalt thou go, and dust shalt thou eat all the days of thy life.

[15] And <u>I</u> will put enmity between thee and the woman, and between thy seed and her Seed; It shall bruise thy head, and thou shalt bruise His heel."

[16] Unto the woman He said, "<u>I</u> will greatly multiply thy sorrow and thy conception. In sorrow thou shalt bring forth children; and thy desire shall be to thy husband, and he shall rule over thee."

[17] And unto Adam He said, "Because thou hast hearkened unto the voice of thy wife, and hast eaten of the tree of which <u>I</u> commanded thee, saying, 'Thou shalt not eat of it,' cursed is the ground for thy sake; in sorrow shalt thou eat of it all the days of thy life.

..............................................................................................................................................

21. Unto Adam also and to his wife did the Lord God make coats of skins, and clothed them.

[22] And <u>the Lord God</u> said, "Behold, the man has become as one of <u>Us,</u> to know good and evil. And now, lest he put forth his hand and take also of the tree of life, and eat and live for ever"

[23] therefore <u>the Lord God</u> sent him forth from the Garden of Eden to till the ground from whence he was taken.

<u>[24] So He drove out the man; and He placed at the east of the Garden of Eden cherubims and a flaming sword which turned every way, to keep the way of the tree of life.</u>

## EXPLANATION

Sin is the transgression of God's law – 1 John 3:4. Read Romans 3:20 and 4:15.

Of course, Adam and Eve transgressed <u>the first commandment</u> of the Ten Commandments. When Adam and Eve chose to obey Satan's words, they ate the forbidden fruit. Thus, they made Satan as their god, instead of the God who created them.

Adam and Eve not only broke the first commandment, but the tenth commandment as well. They coveted to eat of the forbidden fruit which did not belong to them. They had all the fruits to eat, yet they went and ate of the forbidden fruit that God instructed them not to eat. . . .

Many people did not know that Adam and Eve broke the first and the tenth Commandment.

The Ten Commandments was an eternal law that existed in heaven before Adam and Eve were created. Remember, sin existed in heaven by Lucifer. Sin would not have existed in heaven if the law did not exist in heaven.

THINK ABOUT THIS: Though the law that says, "Thou shalt not commit adultery," existed in heaven, however, there was no marriage in heaven. . . . It was God who defined the law without marriage in heaven. God knows the end from the beginning and he made the law before he created heaven and earth – Genesis 1:1.

## NO IMMORTAL SINNERS

After Adam and Eve sinned, GOD did <u>not</u> allow them to eat of <u>"the tree of life"</u> to avoid them becoming <u>immortal sinners</u>.

## THE CONTRADICTION

Today, most people AND Churches teach that "babies are born sinners from Adam and Eve." This notion contradicted the truth. They have made Babies become <u>IMMORTAL SINNERS</u> from birth till death, and till the last baby on earth.

Why should babies become the Sin Bearer for Adam and Eve when JESUS was the only Sin Bearer for Adam and Eve?

No sin of Adam and Eve was transferred to Adam and Eve and their descendants – (Ezekiel 18:20). All sins of Adam and Eve were transferred to JESUS, the only Sin Bearer. HE is the Sin Bearer for all mankind.

# CHAPTER 3

# THE TEN COMMANDMENTS EXISTED IN HEAVEN BEFORE ADAM AND EVE WERE CREATED.

////////////////////////////////////////////////////////////////////////////////////////////////////////////////////////////////////////////

## EXPLANATION

First, we need to define sin in order to understand that the Ten Commandments existed in heaven.

## WHAT IS SIN?

**Scripture: 1 John 3:4 (KJV)**

[4] Whosoever committeth sin transgresseth also the law, for sin is the transgression of the law.

........................................................................................................................................

**Scripture: Isaiah 14:12-14 (KJV)**

[12] "How art thou fallen from heaven, O Lucifer, son of the morning! How art thou cut down to the ground, who didst weaken the nations!

[13] For thou hast said in thine heart, 'I will ascend into heaven, I will exalt my throne above the stars of God; I will sit also upon the mount of the congregation, in the sides of the north.

[14] I will ascend above the heights of the clouds; I will be like the Most High.'

........................................................................................................................................

In order for sin to exist, the Ten Commandments had to be in existence before someone transgresses one of the commandments. Therefore, when Lucifer sinned against God in heaven (Isaiah 14:12-14; Ezekiel 28:12-14), that proves that the Ten Commandments were in existence. Lucifer would not have been a sinner if the Ten Commandments were not in existence in heaven.

........................................................................................................................................

| THE TRUTH | versus | THE LIE |
|---|---|---|

**THE TRUTH**
- Sin is the transgression of GOD'S law – 1 John 3:4.
- GOD created NO baby sinners from Adam.

**THE LIE**
- Sin is by Nature.
- Babies are born sinners.
- Sin is inherited from Adam.

Compiled by: Metusela F. Albert

# CHAPTER 4

# JESUS WROTE THE TEN COMMANDMENTS AT MT. SINAI.

Most Professed Christians believed that God wrote the Ten Commandments on Mt. Sinai and gave through Moses. They did <u>not</u> know that it was JESUS who wrote it on two tablets of stone. Actually, JESUS was that YAHWEH who wrote those commandments. You can only understand it if you read the Scriptures in the CONTEXT and CHRONOLOGICAL ORDER by GOD'S grace. <u>As we grow spiritually, we suppose to grow in our understanding of Scripture.</u> And when we come to understand that JESUS was the Almighty God of Abraham who spoke to Moses at the burning bush *(Exodus 3:13-14; John 8:56-58), we take the truth that enlightened us and throw away old beliefs that are wrong.

## TRUTH IS <u>NOT</u> PROGRESSIVE

The Truth is always the truth. JESUS was the GOD (YAHWEH / JEHOVAH) who created heaven and earth in six days and rested on the seventh day – (Genesis 1:31; 2:1-3). When He wrote the Ten Commandments at Mount. Sinai, the Jews were reminded of the GOD who made heaven and earth - thus, worship is due to Him. Therefore, they were reminded to keep holy the SABBATH day of the LORD. The SABBATH day is a reminder of Creation by GOD, not a reminder of the resurrection day. Of course, the Sabbath day was given to Adam and Eve, well before the New Testament era.

## KNOWLEDGE IS PROGRESSIVE –

We grow in our knowledge of the truth. For example, we may believe something at a certain time, but later change to believe something else when truth is understood better. For example, there was a time I did not know the Sabbath day. I used to believe that Sunday is the Sabbath day.

Therefore, our <u>knowledge of the truth is progressive</u>, but the truth is <u>not</u> progressive. The truth does not change. We are the ones that should change (progress) in our knowledge of the truth. Yes, we should change our beliefs when we become more enlightened. I hope this Book will help some to progress in their knowledge of the truth, if they have not understood yet that the Sabbath day of the LORD is Saturday, not Sunday.

A lot of people get confused and don't know the difference between PROGRESSIVE KNOWLEDGE from THE TRUTH.

## THE TRUTH

JESUS was the Almighty GOD of Abraham, Isaac, and Jacob called – "<u>I AM THAT I AM</u>" who spoke to Moses at the burning bush. He delivered the children of Israel from slavery in Egypt – (Exodus 3:13-14; 20:1-3; John 8:56-58).

HE was YAHWEH (JEHOVAH) who wrote the Ten Commandments on two tablets of stone at Mount Sinai, and gave through Moses – (Exodus 20:1-17; 31:18).

In the New Testament, JESUS said in John 14:15 – "If you love Me, keep My commandments." He was the Father of the children of Israel who wrote the Ten Commandments. Back then, JESUS was <u>not</u> the Son of God. This point needs to be understood well.

## JESUS WAS GOD THE FATHER WHO BECAME THE SON OF GOD <u>BY INCARNATION</u> THROUGH MARY AT BETHLEHEM.

1.   YAHWEH DID <u>NOT</u> HAVE A SON CALLED – JESUS, IN HEAVEN.
2.   YAHWEH DID <u>NOT</u> HAVE A SON CALLED – JESUS, IN THE OLD TESTAMENT ERA.
3.   YAHWEH GAVE BIRTH TO <u>NO SON</u> CALLED – JESUS.
4.   THE GOD OF ABRAHAM HAD <u>NO</u> SON OF GOD CALLED JESUS.
5.   THE HOLY SPIRIT WAS <u>THE SPIRIT OF JESUS</u>, NOT A THIRD PERSON IN HEAVEN.

YAHWEH (JEHOVAH) later took up human flesh by INCARNATION through Mary at Bethlehem and was called - JESUS, the Son of God. Emmanuel became human flesh at Bethlehem – (Isaiah 9:6; 7:14; Matthew 1:21-23; Luke 1:35).

The Ten Commandments are His law. HE gave them. HE was the FATHER in Spirit form who INCARNATED and became visible in human flesh, and died at Calvary as our Sin-Bearer / Redeemer / Savior.

////////////////////////////////////////////////////////////////////////////////////////////////////////////////////////////

..............................................................................................................................

# THE FIRST COMMANDMENT

- Exodus 20:1-3

**THIS IS NOT A TRINITY GOD**

- 1. And <u>God</u> spoke all these words, saying:

- 2 "<u>I am **the LORD thy God**</u>, who have brought thee out of the land of Egypt, out of the house of bondage.

- 3 "<u>Thou shalt have no other gods before Me</u>

# THE SABBATH COMMANDMENT IN THE TEN COMMANDMENTS.

- Exodus 20:8-11

- 8 "<u>Remember the Sabbath day, to keep it holy.</u>

- 9 Six days shalt thou labor and do all thy work;

- 10 <u>but the seventh day is the Sabbath of the LORD thy God</u>. In it thou shalt not do any work, thou, nor thy son, nor thy daughter, thy manservant, nor thy maidservant, nor thy cattle, nor thy stranger that is within thy gates.

- 11 <u>For in six days the LORD made heaven and earth, the sea, and all that in them is, and rested the seventh day. Therefore the LORD blessed the Sabbath day and hallowed it.</u>

# CHAPTER 5

# THE TWO GREAT PRINCIPLES ABOUT LOVE

The Ten Commandments can be found in Exodus 20:1-17.

Exodus 20:1-17 (King James Version).

1. And <u>God spoke</u> all these words, saying:

[2] "<u>I am the LORD THY GOD</u>, who have brought thee out of the land of Egypt, out of the house of bondage.

[3] "Thou shalt have no other gods before Me.

[4] "Thou shalt not make unto thee any graven image, or any likeness of anything that is in heaven above, or that is in the earth beneath, or that is in the water under the earth.

[5] Thou shalt not bow down thyself to them, nor serve them; for I, the LORD THY GOD, AM A JEALOUS GOD, VISITING THE INIQUITY OF THE FATHERS UPON THE CHILDREN UNTO THE THIRD AND FOURTH GENERATION OF THEM THAT HATE ME,

[6] and showing mercy unto thousands of them that love Me and keep My commandments.

[7] "Thou shalt not take the name of the LORD THY GOD IN VAIN, FOR THE LORD WILL NOT HOLD HIM GUILTLESS THAT TAKETH HIS NAME IN VAIN.

[8] "Remember the Sabbath day, to keep it holy.

[9] Six days shalt thou labor and do all thy work;

[10] but the seventh day is the Sabbath of the LORD THY GOD. IN IT THOU SHALT NOT DO ANY WORK, THOU, NOR THY SON, NOR THY DAUGHTER, THY MANSERVANT, NOR THY MAIDSERVANT, NOR THY CATTLE, NOR THY STRANGER THAT IS WITHIN THY GATES.

[11] For in six days the LORD MADE HEAVEN AND EARTH, THE SEA, AND ALL THAT IN THEM IS, AND RESTED THE SEVENTH DAY. THEREFORE THE LORD BLESSED THE SABBATH DAY AND HALLOWED IT.

[12] "Honor thy father and thy mother, that thy days may be long upon the land which the LORD THY GOD GIVETH THEE.

[13] "Thou shalt not kill.

[14] "Thou shalt not commit adultery.

[15] "Thou shalt not steal.

[16] "Thou shalt not bear false witness against thy neighbor.

[17] "Thou shalt not covet thy neighbor's house; thou shalt not covet thy neighbor's wife, nor his manservant, nor his maidservant, nor his ox, nor his ass, nor anything that is thy neighbor's."

...................................................................................................................

The law of God is expressed in <u>two great principles of love</u>.

1. Love God with all thy heart.
2. Love thy neighbor as thyself.

...................................................................................................................

Yes, the first thing for us as sinners is to love God. Without loving God, we cannot love our neighbor. Our love for God comes first, then followed by our love toward our neighbors.

The first four commandments of the Ten Commandments are supposed to be our love toward God.

## THE FIRST FOUR COMMANDMENTS

- Exodus 20:1-17 (King James Version).
- 1. And God spoke all these words, saying:
- [2] "I am the LORD thy God, who have brought thee out of the land of Egypt, out of the house of bondage.

**COMMANDMENT # 1**

- [3] "Thou shalt have no other gods before Me.

**COMMANDMENT # 2**

- [4] "Thou shalt not make unto thee any graven image, or any likeness of anything that is in heaven above, or that is in the earth beneath, or that is in the water under the earth. Thou shalt not bow down thyself to them, nor serve them; for I, the LORD thy God, am a jealous God, visiting the iniquity of the fathers upon the children unto the third and fourth generation of them that hate Me, and showing mercy unto thousands of them that love Me and keep My commandments.

**COMMANDMENT # 3**

- [7] "Thou shalt not take the name of the LORD thy God in vain, for the LORD will not hold him guiltless that taketh His name in vain.

**COMMANDMENT # 4**

- [8] "Remember the Sabbath day, to keep it holy. Six days shalt thou labor and do all thy work; [10] but the seventh day is the Sabbath of the LORD thy God. In it thou shalt not do any work, thou, nor thy son, nor thy daughter, thy manservant, nor thy maidservant, nor thy cattle, nor thy stranger that is within thy gates. For in six days the LORD made heaven and earth, the sea, and all that in them is, and rested the seventh day. Therefore the LORD blessed the Sabbath day and hallowed it.

Compiled by: Metusela F. Albert

And the last six commandments of the Ten Commandments are supposed to be our love toward our neighbor.

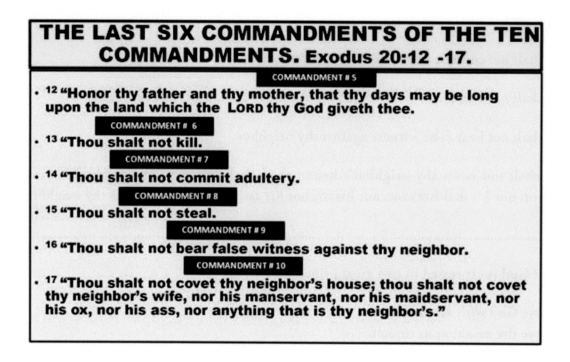

For example, if we love God, we would love to obey his Sabbath Commandment which is the fourth Commandment in the Ten Commandments.

Another example, If we love our neighbor, we would not tell lies about our neighbor or kill our neighbor.

That is the reason God wrote the Ten Commandments in two tablets of stone – the first four Commandments on one stone, and the last six Commandments on the second stone – Exodus 31:18.

Therefore, when JESUS died at Calvary, he did not abolish any commandment. Not even the Sabbath commandment. He did not change the Sabbath from the seventh day of the week to the first day of the week. The Sabbath remains the same in every generation and era beginning from the time of Adam and Eve at creation. Satan will try and change it through false teachings by people. JESUS warned us not to be deceived by false prophets – Matthew 24:3.

That is the reason this book is written for your understanding of the Sabbath day which is Saturday, not Sunday nor any other day of the week.

We are not to worship the Seventh day, but the LORD GOD who gave us the Sabbath day. We are to love God and observe his Sabbath day. Faith leads us to obey God. Faith and works (obedience) go hand in hand. Remember, Faith without obedience is DEAD. James 2:17.

# CHAPTER 6

# THE LAST SABBATH OF JESUS ON EARTH BEFORE HIS DEATH.

**Where did JESUS spend his last Sabbath before his death on the PASSOVER day, the 14TH day of Nisan?**

........................................................................................................................

- John 11 records <u>the resurrection of LAZARUS</u> from the tomb after 4 days of death.
- John 12 records the <u>last Sabbath of JESUS</u> at the home of Mary, Martha, and Lazarus.
- John 13 records the <u>last Communion</u> of JESUS with the disciples on a Thursday evening before his death on a Friday afternoon.

........................................................................................................................

**LET'S READ JOHN 12:1-16**

1. Then Jesus, <u>six days before the Passover</u>, came to Bethany where Lazarus was, who had been dead and whom He had raised from the dead.

² There they made Him a supper; and Martha served, but Lazarus was one of those who sat at the table with Him.

³ Then Mary took a pound of ointment of spikenard, very costly, and anointed the feet of Jesus and wiped His feet with her hair; and the house was filled with the odor of the ointment.

⁴ Then one of His disciples, Judas Iscariot, Simon's son who was to betray Him, said,

⁵ "Why was not this ointment sold for three hundred pence and given to the poor?"

⁶ This he said, not that he cared for the poor, but because he was a thief, and had the money bag and took what was put therein.

[7] Then Jesus said, "Let her alone; against the day of My burying hath she kept this.

[8] For the poor always ye have with you, but Me ye have not always."

[9] Many people of the Jews therefore knew that He was there. And they came not for Jesus' sake only, but that they might see Lazarus also, whom He had raised from the dead.

[10] But the chief priests consulted, that they might put Lazarus also to death,

[11] because by reason of him many of the Jews went away and believed in Jesus.

[12] On the next day many people who had come to the feast, when they heard that Jesus was coming to Jerusalem,

[13] took branches of palm trees and went forth to meet Him and cried, "Hosanna! Blessed is the King of Israel that cometh in the name of the Lord!"

[14] And Jesus, when He had found a young ass, sat thereon, as it is written:

[15] "Fear not, daughter of Zion; behold, thy King cometh, sitting on an ass's colt."

[16] These things His disciples understood not at first; but when Jesus was glorified, then they remembered that these things were written of Him, and that they had done these things unto Him.

........................................................................................................................

## ANOTHER PROOF ABOUT THE SABBATH DAY

- **LET'S FIND OUT THE LAST SABBATH OF JESUS ON EARTH BEFORE HIS DEATH.**
- **Where did JESUS spend his last Sabbath before his death on the PASSOVER day, the 14TH day of Nisan?**
- ........................................................................................................................
- John 11 records the resurrection of LAZARUS from the tomb after 4 days of death.
- John 12 records the last Sabbath of JESUS at the home of Mary, Martha, and Lazarus.
- John 13 records the last Communion of JESUS with the disciples on a Thursday evening before his death on a Friday afternoon.
- **NOTE: THE SABBATH WAS SATURDAY, THE DAY AFTER HIS DEATH ON FRIDAY.**

Compiled by: Metusela F. Albert

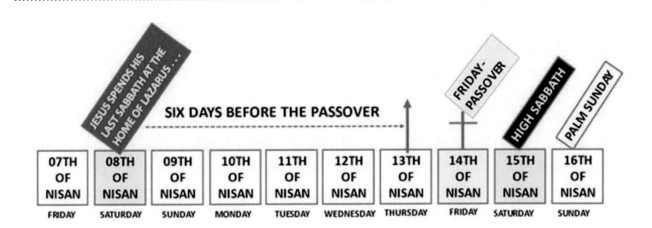

Read – John 12:1-3

1. Then Jesus, six days before the Passover came to Bethany where Lazarus was, who had been dead and whom He had raised from the dead.

[2] There they made Him a supper; and Martha served, but Lazarus was one of those who sat at the table with Him.

[3] Then Mary took a pound of ointment of spikenard, very costly, and anointed the feet of Jesus and wiped His feet with her hair; and the house was filled with the odor of the ointment.

# WHY IS IT IMPORTANT FOR US TO CLARIFY THE SABBATH DAY?

It is important because the Sabbath day is <u>the fourth Commandment</u> in the Ten Commandments. It is <u>part</u> of the Ten Commandments.

Firstly, the Sabbath day reminds us of the GOD who created us, thus worship is due to him – (Revelation 14:6-9).

Secondly, we will all be judged by the Ten Commandments – (Ecclesiastes 12:13-14).

Thirdly, whosoever transgresses one commandment in the Ten Commandments will not be saved – (James 2:10).

Fourthly, if we professed to love JESUS, then we ought to obey his Ten Commandments – (John 14:15).

Fifthly, we are liars and of the devil, if we do not obey his Commandments – (1 John 2:4-6, 1 John 3:4-9).

NOTE: The Ten Commandments are <u>not</u> the Savior. But we cannot be saved by JESUS if we continue to transgress his Commandments. There is no such thing as unconditional salvation. Of course, God loves us unconditionally. But salvation is conditional.

# CONCLUSION

JESUS is the <u>only God</u> in heaven. He alone created heaven and earth in six days and rested on the seventh day. The seventh day is called – SABBATH. The fourth commandment in the Ten Commandments is about the seventh day. This day comes once a week, and over 50 times in a year. This is <u>not</u> an annual day nor celebrated once a year like the Passover Sabbath. The weekly Sabbath day reminds us of God (Yahweh / Jehovah) who created heaven and earth in six literal days, thus worship is due to him alone. This God (YAHWEH) who created heaven and earth was <u>not</u> a Trinity God. Of course, JESUS is <u>not</u> a Trinity God.

JESUS was the Father of the children of Israel in the Old Testament who later incarnated into human flesh. He humbly took up the role of the Son of God through Mary at Bethlehem to die at Calvary as our Sin Bearer / Savior / Redeemer.

NOTE: The Holy Spirit is the Spirit of God which is also the Spirit of JESUS. Try and understand this well. JESUS is the person; the Holy Spirit is <u>not</u> the person. JESUS and the Holy Spirit are <u>not</u> two distinct beings.

There was <u>no</u> Son of God in heaven called JESUS before the angels existed because JESUS was the YAHWEH / JEHOVAH who spoke to the prophets in the Old Testament before his incarnation into human flesh at Bethlehem through Mary around 04 B.C.

There was no such thing as God the Father had a begotten Son in heaven called JESUS. And there was no such thing as God's Son became human flesh.

It was YAHWEY who incarnated into human flesh through Mary at Bethlehem and became the Son of God called JESUS.

////////////////////////////////////////////////////////////////////////////////////////////////////////////

## Genesis 1:1 . . . Which one is CORRECT?

1. In the beginning God created the heaven and earth. **CORRECT**

2. In the beginning the Son of God created heaven and earth. **WRONG**

3. In the beginning the Spirit of God created heaven and earth. **WRONG**

4. In the beginning the Holy Spirit created heaven and earth. **WRONG**

5. In the beginning God the Father, God the Son, and God the Holy Spirit created heaven and earth. **WRONG**

COMPILED BY: METUSELA F. ALBERT

## THE SEVENTH DAY OF THE WEEK IS THE SABBATH DAY. . . .
(Genesis 2:1-3; Exodus 20:8-11).
## JESUS IS THE LORD OF THE SABBATH DAY.

## NO TRINITY GOD CREATED THE SABBATH DAY.

- Genesis 2:1-3 King James Version
- 1. Thus the heavens and the earth were finished, and <u>all the host of them</u>.
- [2] And on <u>the seventh day</u> God ended <u>his</u> work which <u>he</u> had made; and <u>he</u> rested on the seventh day from all <u>his</u> work which <u>he</u> had made.
- [3] And God blessed the seventh day, and sanctified it: because that in it <u>he</u> had rested from all <u>his</u> work which <u>God</u> created and made.

Further Reading: Mark 2:27-28; Luke 4:16; 23:54-56; 24:1-5; Revelation 14:6-7; 22:14; Ecclesiastes 12:13-14.

////////////////////////////////////////////////////////////////////////////////////////////////////////////

- **JESUS WAS THE GOD (ELOHIM / YAHWEH / JEHOVAH) WHO WROTE THE TEN COMMANDMENTS.**
-
- **Scripture:**
-
- **Exodus 20:1-3**
- **1. And God spake all these words, saying,**
-
- **² I am the LORD thy God, which have brought thee out of the land of Egypt, out of the house of bondage.**
-
- **³ Thou shalt have no other gods before me.**

**THIS WAS NOT A TRINITY GOD. . .Look at the Singular PRONOUN.**

////////////////////////////////////////////////////////////////////////////////////////////////////////

**THE GOD WHO SPOKE TO PROPHET ISAIAH IS THE ONLY ONE GOD IN HEAVEN. HE IS JESUS!**

- Isaiah 43:10
- **¹⁰ Ye are my witnesses, saith the LORD, and my servant whom I have chosen: that ye may know and believe me, and understand that I am he: before me there was no God formed, neither shall there be after me.**

**ONLY ONE GOD**

- Isaiah 44:6, 24.
- **⁶ Thus saith the LORD the King of Israel, and his redeemer the LORD of hosts; I am the first, and I am the last; and beside me there is no God.**

**THE REDEEMER IS THE CREATOR, THE FIRST AND THE LAST.**

- **²⁴ Thus saith the LORD, thy redeemer, and he that formed thee from the womb, I am the LORD that maketh all things; that stretcheth forth the heavens alone; that spreadeth abroad the earth by myself;**

- Isaiah 49:16

**THE PROPHECY OF HIS DEATH AT CALVARY**

- **¹⁶ Behold, I have graven thee upon the palms of my hands ; thy walls are continually before me.**

**THIS IS NOT A TRINITY GOD NOR A TRIUNE GOD**

////////////////////////////////////////////////////////////////////////////////////////////////////////

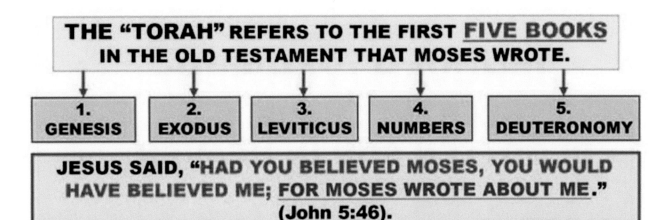

**THE "TORAH" REFERS TO THE FIRST <u>FIVE BOOKS</u> IN THE OLD TESTAMENT THAT MOSES WROTE.**

| 1. GENESIS | 2. EXODUS | 3. LEVITICUS | 4. NUMBERS | 5. DEUTERONOMY |
|---|---|---|---|---|

**JESUS SAID, "HAD YOU BELIEVED MOSES, YOU WOULD HAVE BELIEVED ME; <u>FOR MOSES WROTE ABOUT ME</u>." (John 5:46).**

**JESUS WAS THE ELOHIM / YAHWEH / JEHOVAH / GOD OF ABRAHAM WHO CREATED HEAVEN AND EARTH IN SIX DAYS AND RESTED ON THE SEVENTH DAY, THAT YOU READ IN THE TORAH.**
**JESUS IS NOT A TRINITY GOD.**

////////////////////////////////////////////////////////////////////////////////////////////////////

**MY NEW BOOK THAT WAS PUBLISHED ON SEPTEMBER 12, 2021**

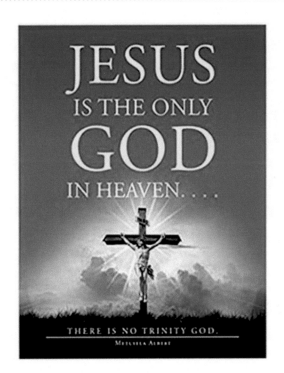

JESUS IS THE ONLY GOD IN HEAVEN. . . .

THERE IS NO TRINITY GOD.
MEULSELA ALBERT

////////////////////////////////////////////////////////////////////////////////////////////////////

# JEHOVAH (YAHWEH) DID **NOT** HAVE A BEGOTTEN SON IN HEAVEN.

## NOTE: Jesus was the Yahweh / Jehovah before his incarnation into human flesh through Mary at Bethlehem.

......................................................................................................................

### THE TRUTH ABOUT GOD, JESUS, AND THE HOLY SPIRIT.... ONLY ONE DIVINE BEING. NOT TWO, AND NOT THREE.

1. JESUS WAS GOD (YAHWEH / JEHOVAH) THE FATHER WHO BECAME THE SON OF GOD <u>BY INCARNATION</u> THROUGH MARY AT BETHLEHEM – (04 B.C.).

2. YAHWEH (JEHOVAH) DID <u>NOT</u> HAVE A SON CALLED – JESUS, IN HEAVEN.

3. YAHWEH (JEHOVAH) DID <u>NOT</u> HAVE A SON CALLED – JESUS, IN THE OLD TESTAMENT ERA.

4. YAHWEH (JEHOVAH) GAVE BIRTH TO NO SON CALLED – JESUS.

5. THE GOD (YAHWEH / JEHOVAH) OF ABRAHAM HAD <u>NO</u> SON CALLED JESUS.

6. SATAN WANTED TO BE LIKE GOD IN HEAVEN, NOT LIKE THE SON OF GOD BECAUSE THERE WAS NO SON OF GOD IN HEAVEN.

7. THE HOLY SPIRIT WAS THE SPIRIT OF GOD, NOT A THIRD PERSON.

Compiled by: Metusela F. Albert

THE SABBATH DAY WAS GIVEN TO ADAM AND EVE AT THE GARDEN OF EDEN TO REMIND THEM OF THE GOD WHO CREATED HEAVEN AND EARTH IN SIX DAYS. . . IT WAS INTENDED TO REMIND THEM AND THEIR GENERATIONS THAT GOD WAS THE CREATOR AND WORSHIP IS DUE TO HIM.

IF THE WORLD HAD REMEMBERED GOD (JESUS) AS THE CREATOR, THERE WOULD HAVE BEEN <u>NO EVOLUTION</u> TEACHING, AND <u>NO TRINITY (TRIUNE) GOD</u> THEORY TEACHING.

OF COURSE, THERE WOULD HAVE BEEN <u>NO DUALITY</u> GOD THEORY.

THE SABBATH DAY WAS <u>NOT</u> A MEMORIAL OF THE RESURRECITON. IN FACT, THE COMMUNION SERVICE WAS THE SERVICE TO REMIND US OF THE DEATH OF JESUS ON THE 14TH DAY OF NISAN, AND HIS RESURRECTION ON THE 16TH DAY OF THE JEWISH MONTH – NISAN / ABIB.

////////////////////////////////////////////////////////////////////////////////////////////////////////////

# WHY IS IT IMPORTANT FOR US TO CLARIFY THE SABBATH DAY?

It is important because the Sabbath day is <u>the fourth Commandment</u> in the Ten Commandments. It is <u>part</u> of the Ten Commandments.

Firstly, the Sabbath day reminds us of the GOD who created us, thus worship is due to him – (Revelation 14:6-9).

Secondly, we will all be judged by the Ten Commandments – (Ecclesiastes 12:13-14).

Thirdly, whosoever transgresses one commandment in the Ten Commandments will not be saved – (James 2:10).

Fourthly, if we professed to love JESUS, then we ought to obey his Ten Commandments – (John 14:15).

Fifthly, we are liars, if we do not obey his Commandments – (1 John 2:4-6).

NOTE: The Ten Commandments are <u>not</u> the Savior. But we cannot be saved by JESUS if we continue to transgress his Commandments. There is no such thing as unconditional salvation. Of course, God loves us unconditionally. But salvation is conditional.

**REMEMBER THIS: During the time of JESUS, the Pharisees tried to keep the Sabbath Commandment but they rejected the LORD of the Sabbath which came in human flesh.**

**Today, most Christians professed to believe in JESUS but rejected the Sabbath Commandment. They are so contradicting. What a Shame!**

//////////////////////////////////////////////////////////////////////////////////////////////////////////////////////////

Printed in the United States
by Baker & Taylor Publisher Services